JAMAICA

AF767156

PEP

Language Arts

Performance Task

GRADE 5

Practice Papers

hachette LEARNING

The Publishers would like to thank the following for permission to reproduce copyright material.

Photo credits

t = top, b = below, l = left, r = right, c = centre, b/g = background

p.7: © Krakenimages.com/stock.adobe.com; p.10: © Wolfilser/stock.adobe.com; p.25: © Grandbrothers/stock.adobe.com; p.28: © Brebca/stock.adobe.com; p.34: (tl) © inna717/stock.adobe.com, (br) © Marcin Kilarski/Wirestock/stock.adobe.com; p.40: (t) © buenaventura13/stock.adobe.com, (c) © Silver/stock.adobe.com, (b) © Asya M/stock.adobe.com; p.50: © Curto/stock.adobe.com; p.51: © chadchai/stock.adobe.com; p.57: © Jacob Lund/stock.adobe.com; p.58: (t) © uckyo/stock.adobe.com, (c) © Angelika Heine/stock.adobe.com, (b) © pilipphoto/stock.adobe.com; p.64: © VectorShop/stock.adobe.com; p.65: © David Brown/stock.adobe.com; p.75: © Gary Dean Clarke/stock.adobe.com; p.84: © Семен Саливанчук/stock.adobe.com; p.88: © Krakenimages.com/stock.adobe.com.
p. 34: 'Being a tree' © Opal Palmer Adisa; p. 34: 'The Greedy Monster' © Irene Rawnsley; p. 50: 'Carrots' © Shel Silverstein.

We have used all reasonable efforts to correctly credit all licensed material in this book. If your material has been mis-credited please contact us so that we can amend the credit for future editions.

Acknowledgements

Although every effort has been made to ensure that website addresses are correct at time of going to press, Hachette Learning cannot be held responsible for the content of any website mentioned in this book. It is sometimes possible to find a relocated web page by typing in the address of the home page for a website in the URL window of your browser.

Hachette UK's policy is to use papers that are natural, renewable and recyclable products and made from wood grown in well-managed forests and other controlled sources. The logging and manufacturing processes are expected to conform to the environmental regulations of the country of origin.

To order, please visit www.HachetteLearning.com or contact Customer Service at education@hachette.co.uk / +44 (0)1235 827827.

ISBN: 9781036005177

First published in 2026 by Hachette Learning (a trading division of Hodder & Stoughton Limited),
An Hachette UK Company
Carmelite House
50 Victoria Embankment
London EC4Y 0DZ

www.HachetteLearning.com

The authorised representative in the EEA is Hachette Ireland, 8 Castlecourt Centre, Dublin 15, D15 XTP3, Ireland (email: info@hbgi.ie)

Impression number 10 9 8 7 6 5 4 3 2 1

Year 2030 2029 2028 2027 2026

Cover photo © GoodStudio- stock.adobe.com

Illustrations by Hyphen S.A./Konstantina Kyratzidou

Typeset by Hyphen S.A.

Printed in Printed and bound in Great Britain by Bell & Bain Ltd, Glasgow

A catalogue record for this title is available from the British Library.

FSC www.fsc.org
MIX
Paper | Supporting responsible forestry
FSC™ C104740

Contents

How to use this book

Think about successful athletes. Athletes learn about their sport, and they practise and train hard to become excellent performers.

You can excel at communication by learning how to identify the purpose and audience for communicating and then training yourself to answer different types of questions.

You are going to work through **Practice paper 1** with your teacher. This will help you to:

- Read questions carefully and work out what type of answer to give.
- Learn how you can get good results even if your answer is different from everybody else's.
- Understand what the different ratings mean and see how you can improve your rating.
- Reflect on your own work to help you see what you did well and what you can improve on in the next task.

Each task in this book has three supporting features.

Before you start …

This section helps you think carefully about questions and what it is you are being asked to do. There are different activities for each task.

Hints

These are given in the task itself to help you think about the questions and how you should answer them. As you progress, there will be fewer hints in the tasks.

Reflection

This section encourages you to think about your own learning and how you can improve on it.

Practice paper 1 also has a section called **How do you know how well you did?**

In this section you will see possible answers to the questions and what rating they were given. The aim of this section is to show you what you need to do to get the best possible results.

Practice paper 1

This task has two parts. For both parts, you must read **Source 1** and **Source 2**.

- Part 1 has questions 1 to 9.
- Part 2 has question 10.

→ Before you start ...

Look at these students' responses for the following question: What is your favourite machine and why? Both students have the right answer, but Annika gets a better grade than Nadia. Can you see why?

Nadia's response	Annika's response
My favourite machine is the phone. It is a device that is small and can do so much. I can use it to make calls, send messages, browse the internet and access social media. It also has a camera, a calculator and other apps that I use on a daily basis.	My favourite machine is the smartphone. It is now an essential device that has revolutionised the way we live, work and communicate. Overall, smartphones have had a profound impact on our lives and may have an even greater impact in the future. They are one of the most important inventions of the 21st century.

Nadia uses simple language, such as, "I can use it to make calls" and "It also has a camera, a calculator".

Nadia's answer focuses on the main points, such as how she uses the phone.

Annika uses more complex language, such as, "It is now an essential device that has revolutionised the way we live".

Annika's answer is more objective and advanced as it states that the smartphone is her favourite machine, as well as stating the benefits as an important invention.

Look at the instruction words and phrases in the Knowledge boxes on the next page. Which Knowledge box goes with Nadia and Annika's responses?

Write **Recalling information**, **Skills and concepts**, **Strategic thinking** or **Extended thinking** next to their name on the next page. Think about what each instruction means in the Knowledge boxes before you answer the question.

Nadia

____

____

Annika

____

____

Recalling information	Skills and concepts	Strategic thinking	Extended thinking
Remember, recall, recognise or locate basic details, ideas. There is one correct answer.	Explain, show relationships; use your skills and what you know to make decisions about what to do and how to do it. There is one correct answer.	Explain your thinking and give reasons for your answers. There are different answers and different ways to find the answers.	Plan, think and put ideas together to solve a problem. There are many possible answers and ways of solving the problem.

Look at the end of the test to check the Knowledge box that goes with Nadia and Annika's responses.

Part 1

Question 1

a What strategies should you use before reading a text to help you understand it well? Circle the answer(s).

i Preview the text by skimming the title, headings and images.

ii Activate your prior knowledge by thinking about what you already know about the topic.

iii Read different texts on a similar topic.

iv Include all of the above.

b What strategies should you use while reading a text to help you understand? Circle the answer(s).

i Ask yourself questions about the text as you read.

ii Highlight relevant points.

iii Ignore the parts of the text that you do not understand.

iv Read the text quickly without paying attention to the details.

c What strategies should you use after reading a text to help you remember and understand what you have read? Circle the answer(s).

i Review your notes and summaries.

ii Discuss the text with others.

iii Reflect on what you have read.

iv Do not think about the text after you have read it.

SOURCE 1

Machines in the Home

1 Machines are tools that assist us in doing a variety of tasks efficiently and effectively. Some machines perform tasks that would be impossible for people to do on their own. Most tasks would take much longer to complete or **they** would be inconvenient to do without machines, so they are essential to our daily lives. Our reliance on them is considerable and life would be difficult without **them**. Machines can be small, like an iPad or a laptop, or they can be large, like a washing machine, dishwasher or fridge-freezer.

2 Machines help us in many ways at home, for example, the refrigerator keeps food fresh and drinks cold. The freezer preserves food and limits food spoilage. Our oven or microwave allows us to cook and heat food quickly. Lighting a campfire every time we need to cook or heat something would be impractical, as **it** would take time and would have to be done by hand. Some common machines used in the home include appliances that help us to:

- prepare and cook food, such as refrigerators, ovens, microwaves, dishwashers and blenders
- clean and dry our clothes, such as washing machines and dryers
- clean our homes, such as vacuum cleaners, mops and brooms
- relax and enjoy ourselves, such as televisions, computers and gaming consoles.

3 Therefore, machines make people's lives easier and more convenient in many ways. **They** help us save time, do tasks that would be difficult to do on our own and help us live more comfortably.

Question 2

Look at these sentences from paragraph 1.

Topic Sentence: Machines are tools that assist us in doing a variety of tasks efficiently and effectively.

Supporting Evidence: Some machines perform tasks that would be impossible for people to do on their own.

> The topic sentence is the main idea of the paragraph. It is usually the first sentence in the paragraph. The supporting sentence provides examples, explains the topic sentence in more detail and gives reasons why the topic sentence is true.

a Look at paragraph 2. Write the topic sentence and the supporting evidence.

Topic Sentence:

____

____

Supporting Evidence:

____

____

b Look at paragraph 3. Write the topic sentence and the supporting evidence.

Topic Sentence:

____

____

Supporting Evidence:

____

____

Question 3

Look at **Source 1** and answer the questions:

a What does the word **they** refer to in paragraph 1?

____

____

b What does the word **them** refer to in paragraph 1?

____

c What does the word **it** refer to in paragraph 2?

____

d What does the word **They** refer to in paragraph 3?

____

Question 4

a Why do we use machines?

____

____

____

b Write two examples of small machines and two examples of large machines.

Small machines	Large machines

c How do machines help us at home?

____

____

____

d What would happen if we did not have machines at home?

____

____

____

SOURCE 2

Machines outside of the Home

Machines outside of the home are employed for transportation, construction, manufacturing, agriculture and many other industries. This makes completion of industrial work more efficient and effective, and using machines makes people's lives easier and more convenient. Some examples of what machines are used for outside of the home are manufacturing, construction, agriculture and transport.

Some machines perform tasks that would be impossible for people to do on their own. Firstly, machines are used to manufacture products such as food, clothes, cars and airplanes to a high standard of quality whilst being produced efficiently. Secondly, they are also essential in the construction industry where excavators, industrial drills, bulldozers and cranes are used to build buildings, roads, bridges and other structures. Thirdly, agriculture is more productive in producing food by using machines such as harvesters, tractors and milk processing equipment. Finally, cars, buses, trains and airplanes transport people and manufactured goods around the world.

In conclusion, machines make it possible for people to travel and products to be transported long distances quickly and easily.

Question 5

For each statement, tick [✔] whether the information is from **Source 1**, **Source 2** or **Both sources**. Tick only one box for each statement.

	Statement	Source 1	Source 2	Both sources
1	Machines make people's lives easier and more convenient in many ways.			
2	Kitchen, cleaning, laundry and entertainment appliances all involve the use of machines.			
3	Machines are used in transportation, construction, manufacturing and agriculture.			
4	We can produce more food using machines.			
5	Machines perform tasks that would be impossible for people to do on their own.			

Question 6

a Sort the words in the vocabulary box into lists according to how we use these machines.

bulldozers refrigerators ovens buses microwaves cranes
dishwashers airplanes blenders harvesters washing machines
tractors dryers vacuum cleaners cars mops brooms
televisions computers trains

Inside the home	Outside the home

b Choose one item that you think could be used inside and outside the home and say why.

Transitional words connect sentences. They help the reader understand the relationships between different ideas. Examples include "first", "second", "third", "next", "then", "afterward", "in addition", "subsequently", "finally", "lastly".

Question 7

Use at least two transitional words from the box in your answers to questions **8a** and **8b**.

Question 8

a Can you think of a machine that has changed the way we live?

____

____

____

b How do you think machines will change in the future?

____

____

____

Question 9

a Identify the simple and complete subject in the following sentences:

Read this sentence and the annotations.

The old, worn-out washing machine loudly cleaned the clothes.

A simple subject is a single word or words representing the main noun without any of its modifiers or adjectives, and tells who or what the sentence is about.

A complete subject represents the simple subject and all the words that go with it.

i The refrigerator in the kitchen keeps the food cold.

Simple subject: ______________________________

Complete subject: ______________________________

ii The water sprinkler in the garden waters the grass.

Simple subject: ______________________________

Complete subject: ______________________________

b Identify the simple and complete predicate in the following sentences:

Read this sentence and the annotations.

The lawnmower in the garden cuts the grass quickly.

The simple predicate is the verb that tells what the subject does or is (cuts).

The complete predicate is the verb and all of the words that go with it (cuts the grass quickly).

ICT and Mathematics link: You could use Google Forms to survey others about how they use machines in their home and create a chart to show results.

i The tumble-dryer in the basement dries our clothes quickly.

Simple predicate: ______________________________

Complete predicate: ______________________________

ii The computers at school are faster than my computer at home.

Simple predicate: ______________________________

Complete predicate: ______________________________

Part 2

Use some transitional words. These will help the reader follow the links between your different ideas.

Question 10

Read the introduction and conclusion of an essay about machines in the future. Complete the essay by writing two paragraphs about:

- what machines will be like *in the home* in the future
- what machines will be like *outside the home* in the future.

Plan

Think of a topic sentence and supporting sentences for each paragraph.

To add information	To contrast information	To show cause and effect	To show time
also, in addition, furthermore, for example, for instance	but, however, nevertheless, on the other hand	as a result, because, consequently, for this reason, so, therefore	before, earlier, finally, first, second, meanwhile, next, now, previously, since, then, until, when, while

Introduction

It is likely that machines will continue to advance in technological capabilities, as they become more sophisticated in the future. They will be able to perform tasks more efficiently than they can today. This will significantly impact life at home and at school or work. This essay will discuss what machines will be like in the home and outside the home in the future.

What machines will be like in the home.

What machines will be like outside the home.

When you write your essay, remember to use details in your own words from **Source 1** and **Source 2** to support your explanation.

Conclusion

Overall, I believe that machines will continue to have a major impact on our lives in the future. They will make our lives easier and more convenient in many ways, but they could also cause some challenges, such as job losses due to automation and safety concerns. It is important to be aware of both the benefits and the challenges of using machines so that we can make decisions about how to use them in the future.

Practice paper 1 Self-evaluation

How do you know how well you did?

Here is the Knowledge box that goes with Nadia and Annika's responses:

Nadia: Skills and concepts
Nadia's response uses her skills and knowledge to identify and write why the smartphone is her favourite machine. Her response is simple and is a direct answer to the question.

Annika: Extended thinking
Annika's response goes beyond the use of skills and understanding basic concepts. She puts together ideas and explains how smartphones have a profound impact on our lives and predicts that they continue to advance in the future.

Part 1

Now that you have worked through Part 1 of Practice paper 1, you are going to look at some answers that students gave to see how they were rated. Then you can rate your own answers using this scale.

Remember: There are often many ways to show understanding. Your response doesn't have to look exactly like the examples to be valid.

1 Beginning	2 Developing	3 Proficient	4 Highly proficient
The student is starting to explore the ideas. They may need more support to show how their answers connect to the topic.	Answers show some evidence that the student partly understands the concepts.	Answers show that the student is competent and understands most of the concepts.	Answers show that the student understands all the concepts very well and may have found the task quite easy.

Different thinkers may reach proficiency in different ways – by writing, drawing, speaking or explaining in their own words.

We will look at answers to the four different levels of questions.

Strategic thinking

Question 1

a What strategies should you use before reading a text to help you understand it better?

(i) Preview the text by skimming the title, headings and images.

(ii) Activate your prior knowledge by thinking about what you already know about the topic.

iii Read different texts on a similar topic.

iv Include all of the above.

b What strategies should you use while reading a text to help you understand?

(i) Ask yourself questions about the text as you read.

(ii) Highlight relevant points.

iii Ignore the parts of the text that you do not understand.

iv Read the text quickly without paying attention to the details.

c What strategies should you use after reading a text to help you remember and understand what you have read?

(i) Review your notes and summaries.

(ii) Discuss the text with others.

(iii) Reflect on what you have read.

iv Do not think about the text after you have read it.

Word Recognition and Fluency:
Identify strategies found most helpful before, during and after reading.

3 Proficient

Students need to think critically about the reading strategies that they find most helpful. To answer these questions, students also need to exercise reasoning skills about their own reading process and to identify the strategies that work best for them.

Skills and concepts

Question 2

a Look at paragraph 2. Write the topic sentence and the supporting evidence.

Topic Sentence:

Machines help us in many ways at home, for example, the refrigerator keeps food fresh and drinks cold.

Supporting Evidence:

The freezer preserves food and limits food spoilage.

b Look at paragraph 3. Write the topic sentence and the supporting evidence.

Topic Sentence:

Therefore, machines make people's lives easier and more convenient in many ways.

Supporting Evidence:

They help us save time, do tasks that would be difficult to do on our own and help us live more comfortably.

Comprehension: Develop an understanding of text organisation and structure to assist in comprehension (topic sentences and supporting sentences).

2 Developing

Shows growing understanding of the topic. The student is beginning to explain how machines affect our lives, with more clarity or support needed.

Recalling information

Question 3

Look at **Source 1** and answer the questions:

a What does the word **they** refer to in paragraph 1? Most tasks

b What does the word **them** refer to in paragraph 1? machines

c What does the word **it** refer to in paragraph 2? Lighting a campfire

d What does the word **They** refer to in paragraph 3? machines

Word Recognition and Fluency:
Apply appropriate word structure to decipher meaning.

1 Beginning

The answers are found explicitly in the text, so the students require a basic understanding of referents (pronouns).

Skills and concepts

Question 4

a Why do we use machines?

Suggested answer:
They assist us in doing a variety of tasks efficiently and effectively.

b Write two examples of small machines and two examples of large machines.

Small: iPad, laptop

Large: washing machine, dishwasher

c How do machines help us at home?

Suggested answer:
Machines make our lives easier and more convenient. For example, they can save time to do tasks that would be difficult to do on our own, and, therefore, allow us to live more comfortably.

d What would happen if we did not have machines at home?

Suggested answer:
Some tasks would be difficult to do as it would take time and be labour intensive.

Comprehension: Develop an understanding of text organisation and structure to assist in comprehension (topic sentences and supporting sentences).

2 Developing

Shows some evidence that the student partly understands the importance of machines in our lives.

Extended thinking

Question 5

For each statement, tick [✔] whether the information is from **Source 1**, **Source 2** or **Both sources**. Tick only one box for each statement.

	Statement	Source 1	Source 2	Both sources
1	Machines make people's lives easier and more convenient in many ways.			✔
2	Kitchen, cleaning, laundry and entertainment appliances all involve the use of machines.	✔		
3	Machines are used in transportation, construction, manufacturing and agriculture.		✔	
4	We can produce more food using machines.		✔	
5	Machines perform tasks that would be impossible for people to do on their own.			✔

Statements 1 and 5	Statement 2
1 Beginning *The student correctly identifies* ***Sources 1*** *and* ***2****. The statements are the exact words in the text.*	2 Developing *The student associates the categories of kitchen, cleaning, laundry and entertainment with the machines mentioned in the text.*
Statement 3	**Statement 4**
1 Beginning *The student correctly identifies* ***Source 2****. The statement is the exact words in the text.*	3 Proficient *The student needs to link the statement "… produce more food …" with "… being produced efficiently …".*

Skills and concepts

Question 6

a Sort the words in the Vocabulary box into lists according to how we use the machines.

Inside the home	Outside the home
refrigerators, ovens, microwaves, dishwashers, blenders, washing machines, tractors, dryers, vacuum cleaners, mops, brooms, televisions, computers	bulldozers, buses, cranes, airplanes, harvesters, cars, trains

b Choose one item that you think could be used inside and outside the home and say why.

Suggested answer:

Computers can be used at home for entertainment and outside the home at school for studies.

Word Recognition and Fluency: Use knowledge of grade level words.
② Developing
The question requires students to understand the different ways that machines are used, and to be able to apply that knowledge to sort the words into the correct lists.

Extended thinking

Question 7

Use at least two transitional words from the box in your answers to questions **8a** and **8b**.

Question 8

a Can you think of a machine that has changed the way we live?

Suggested answers:

Grammar and Conventions: Use appropriate transitional words in written communication.	
The washing machine has changed the way we live. **First,** it makes cleaning clothes easy. **Second,** it is quicker than hand washing. **Third,** it frees up our time to do other things.	The washing machine has changed the way we live. **First,** it has freed up our time and **subsequently** we can do things, such as study or spend time with our families. **Second,** we have cleaner clothes than hand washing which can improve our health and well-being. **Third,** it allows us to care for our clothes, which can extend their lifespan and save us money.
② Developing *Requires students to apply their knowledge of the washing machine and the impact it has on our lives using simple transitional words.*	④ Highly proficient *The response provides a comprehensive well-reasoned explanation of how the washing machine has changed the way we live. It also supports its claims with evidence, such as the fact that washing machines free up our time, make our clothes cleaner and make it easier to care for our clothes.*

b How do you think machines will change in the future?

Suggested answers:

Grammar and Conventions: Use appropriate transitional words in written communication.	
I think machines will become more intelligent and more integrated into our lives in the future. **For example,** they will be used to automate tasks that are currently done by humans. **In addition,** they will also be used to develop new products and services.	Machines are changing the world at an unprecedented pace. In the future, I think machines will become even more intelligent and beneficial to humans. **For example,** AI-powered medical devices could diagnose diseases early. **In addition,** self-driving cars could revolutionise transportation and make our roads safer. **Finally,** robotics could automate manufacturing, further freeing up workers to focus on more creative work.
3 Proficient *The response shows a good understanding of the question. It uses simple, but appropriate transitional words whilst also using a high level of vocabulary such as "integrated" and "automate".*	4 Highly proficient *The response provides a comprehensive, well-reasoned explanation of how machines will change in the future. It also supports its claims with evidence, such as AI-powered machines, self-driving cars and the use of robotics. Appropriate transitional words are used to support the fluency of the text.*

Recalling information

Question 9

a Identify the simple and complete subject in the following sentences:

i The refrigerator in the kitchen keeps the food cold.

Simple subject: refrigerator

Complete subject: The refrigerator in the kitchen

ii The water sprinkler in the garden waters the grass.

Simple subject: water sprinkler

Complete subject: The water sprinkler in the garden

b Identify the simple and complete predicate in the following sentences:

i The tumble-dryer in the basement dries our clothes quickly.

Simple predicate: dries

Complete predicate: dries our clothes quickly

ii The computers at school are faster than my computer at home.

Simple predicate: are

Complete predicate: are faster than my computer at home

Grammar and Conventions: Distinguish between the simple and complete subject and predicate in sentences.

2 Developing

The answers require students to recall the definitions of simple and complete subjects and predicates, and to apply that knowledge to identify these parts of speech in the given sentences.

Part 2

Question 10

Task 1 You are going to write two paragraphs of an essay about:

- what machines will be like *in the home* in the future.
- what machines will be like *outside the home* in the future.

Suggested answer:

What machines will be like in the home in future

In the future, machines in the home will be able to learn people's daily routine and anticipate their needs. **For example**, if you run out of milk, the refrigerators may be able to track what is in the fridge and automatically order more. **In addition**, washing machines may be able to detect the type of program needed depending on the clothes placed in the machine. **Furthermore**, robots may be able to carry out domestic tasks, such as cleaning and cooking.

What machines will be like outside the home in the future

Machines outside the home in the future will become more advanced. **For example**, self-driving cars which have already been invented may be able to fly. **Consequently**, transportation for people and for delivery of products will be easier than now. **Finally**, robots may be used to build buildings and do tasks that are too dangerous for humans.

Writing: Use knowledge of the writing process. Locate and organise information to create well-constructed paragraphs.
❹ Highly proficient
*This response goes beyond simply recalling facts and definitions to explain and analyse the potential impact of machines on our lives in the future. For example, 1) "… automatically order more." 2) "**Consequently**, transportation for people and for delivery of products will be easier than now." This response also considers different perspectives on the use of machines.*

Reflection

Complete this flow chart.

My strengths

Evidence of my strengths

My goals for the next performance task

My plan to reach the goals

Practice paper 2

This task has two parts. For both parts, you must read **Source 1** and **Source 2**.

- Part 1 has questions 1 to 8.
- Part 2 has question 9.

→ Before you start ...

- Read through all the questions.
- Underline the question words (where, how, what etc.).
- Think about how you can answer each question.

Part 1

Question 1

Look at the compound noun "air fryer" and explain what you think it means.

____

SOURCE 1

Air fryers, the healthier option

1 Air fryers have become increasingly popular in recent years for several reasons. Firstly, you can cook a wide variety of foods with limited fat, secondly, they are smaller than most kitchen ovens and finally, **they** are easy to use.

2 Air fryers circulate hot air around your food, which cooks **it** without the need for a lot of oil. This means that fried foods, like fries, chicken nuggets and battered fish, can be cooked without all the extra fat and calories.

3 In addition to being healthier, air fryers are safe to use and less dangerous than traditional deep fat fryers **which** can be a fire hazard. There is no need to heat up a lot of oil and there is less mess to clean up afterwards.

4 If you follow **these** suggestions, you will get the best results. Before cooking, preheat the air fryer, cut food into small, similar-sized pieces and avoid overcrowding the basket. During cooking, shake or toss food halfway through to prevent uneven cooking.

Here are just a few of the benefits of using an air fryer:

- Healthy cooking: Air fryers use up to 90% less oil than traditional frying, so you can enjoy your food without extra fat and calories.
- Convenience: Air fryers are easy to use and clean.
- Versatile: Air fryers can be used to cook a wide variety of foods, including chicken nuggets, battered fish and frozen vegetables.
- Affordable: Whilst good quality air fryers are still expensive, they are likely to become cheaper as their popularity increases.

If you are keen on cooking healthy food in a more convenient way, an air fryer is the perfect solution. Try one today and see for yourself!

Question 2

What is the purpose of the text?

Question 3

a How does an air fryer work?

b What are two main benefits of using an air fryer?

c What are some of the foods that can be cooked in an air fryer?

Question 4

Look at **Source 1** and answer the questions:

a What does the word **they** refer to in paragraph 1? ____________________

b What does the word **it** refer to in paragraph 2? ____________________

c What does the word **which** refer to in paragraph 3? ____________________

d What does the word **these** refer to in paragraph 4? ____________________

Question 5

Look at the words in the table. For each one, write its root word, prefix and/or suffix where there is white space in the table to do so. Some of the words have been transformed as examples.

A root word is a word or word part that can be transformed into new words by attaching prefixes before it and/or suffixes after it. Understanding the meanings of root words can help you work out the meanings of new words.

Word	Root	Prefix	Suffix
reheat	heat	re	
crumbly			
affordable			
uneven			
portable	port		able
unhealthy			
return			
thickly	thick		ly
remove			

Question 6

a What does the prefix *re-* mean? Circle the answer.

i back — ii forward

iii behind — iv below

b What does the prefix *un-* mean? Circle the answer.

i no — ii never

iii not — iv neither

c What does the suffix *-able* mean? Circle the answer.

i can — ii cannot

iii must — iv should

Nouns are naming words, for example, "cat", "tree", "man".

Adverbs modify verbs, adjectives or other adverbs. For example, in the sentence "She runs quickly", "quickly" is the adverb.

Adjectives describe nouns, for example, "red", "big", "round".

Verbs describe actions, for example, "run", "jump", "skip".

d What type of words are *thickly* and *crumbly*? Circle the answer.

i nouns

ii adverbs

iii adjectives

iv verbs

SOURCE 2

The kitchen oven versus the air fryer

While air fryers have grown in popularity, conventional kitchen ovens have several advantages over them.

- **Versatility:** Conventional ovens can cook a wide variety of foods, including meats, vegetables, baked goods and casseroles. Air fryers are typically limited to cooking smaller items, such as chicken nuggets, French fries and frozen vegetables.
- **Cooking time:** Conventional ovens can cook food more quickly than air fryers, especially if the oven is preheated. Air fryers can be slower to cook food, especially if the basket is overcrowded.
- **Even cooking:** Conventional ovens can cook food more evenly than air fryers. Air fryers can sometimes leave food unevenly cooked, especially if the basket is overcrowded.
- **Capacity:** Conventional ovens have a larger capacity than air fryers. This means that you can cook larger meals and several dishes simultaneously in a conventional oven, but air fryers are typically limited to cooking smaller meals or individual portions.
- **Price:** Conventional ovens are typically less expensive than air fryers although air fryers are becoming cheaper.

Overall, conventional kitchen ovens are more versatile, efficient and affordable than air fryers. However, air fryers may be a good option for people who are looking for a way to cook healthier meals or who have limited counter space.

In this context, "versatility" means having lots of different ways of being used.

ICT and science link: You could create a simple online poll (e.g. Google Forms or Microsoft Forms) asking classmates which appliance they think cooks food more evenly, and why. Present your findings in a bar chart.

Question 7

a Explain how the versatility of conventional kitchen ovens makes them a more efficient choice than air fryers.

____

____

____

b Compare and contrast the even cooking capabilities of conventional kitchen ovens and air fryers.

____

____

____

c Evaluate the positives and negatives of using a conventional kitchen oven or an air fryer for a family of four.

____

____

____

Question 8

How would you conduct an experiment to test the cooking time and evenness of cooking chicken nuggets in a conventional kitchen oven and in an air fryer? Use transitional words where possible in your response. For example: *first*, *second*, *third*, *then*, *finally* etc.

____

____

____

____

Part 2

Question 9

Write an essay which includes three paragraphs: an introduction, a main body and a conclusion. Use:

- the information in **Sources 1** and **2** to determine in your opinion which is better, a kitchen cooker or an air fryer
- the points below to guide you in writing each part of your essay.

Introduction

- Start with a hook: open with something that will grab the reader's attention.
- State the purpose of your writing: this should be a clear statement of what you are trying to achieve in your essay.

Main body

- Highlight the similarities and differences between the two sources and explain how this information helps you to determine which appliance is better.
- State your opinion on which appliance is better. Provide a clear explanation of your reasons.

Conclusion

- Restate your opinion on which appliance is better and provide a brief summary of the reasons for your opinion.

Use some transitional words that will help the reader follow the links between your ideas, such as: "for example", "also", "in addition", "furthermore", "consequently", "for this reason".

When you write your essay, remember to use details in your own words from **Source 1** and **Source 2** to support your explanation.

Reflection

Answer these questions once you have completed the task.

- What evidence shows that I have achieved my aims?

___

___

___

- What did I do well?

___

___

___

- What can I improve on?

___

___

___

Practice paper 3

This task has two parts. For both parts, you must read **Source 1** and **Source 2**.

- Part 1 has questions 1 to 8.
- Part 2 has question 9.

→ Before you start ...

- Circle or highlight all the instruction words.
- Underline any words that tell you to give a reason for your answers.
- Some questions are open-ended. That means there is more than one way to answer.
- It is important to explain your answer where possible.

Part 1

Question 1

a Before reading, what can you see and hear around you?

____

____

b Think of **two** things that you need from the environment.

____

____

c Think of **two** things that the environment needs from you.

____

____

SOURCE 1

Being a tree

One time
I stood on the arm of the sofa
balancing on one leg
my arms spread wide
like branches.

I was a gigantic tree
in the deep green forest.
Many birds sat on my branches
chirping their happy songs.
Small animals nestled by my trunk
prancing and playing, being free.
And just as a blue jay
was about to land on my branch
Mom shouted, 'Be careful!'
The blue jay flew away.
I fell, and my tree toppled over.

By Opal Palmer Adisa

SOURCE 2

The Greedy Monster

A greedy monster
came and ate
the leaves from the trees.

The wind was sad.
He had no one
to tickle with his breeze.

The greedy monster
came and ate
the branches, every bit.

The birds flew, sulky,
in the sky;
they had nowhere to sit.

The monster
ate the forest,
trunks and roots, in a day.

Now houses stand where the forest stood
and the birds have gone away.

By Irene Rawnsley

ICT link: You could create a short video of yourself pretending to be a tree. Use gestures and sound effects. Add text or voice to describe your forest scene.

Question 2

What do you think the poet's purpose is in **Source 1**, *Being a tree*?

Question 3

a How does the poet describe the tree in the poem? What makes the tree "gigantic"?

b How did the poem make you feel when the blue jay flew away and the tree toppled over? Why do you think that happened?

Similes and metaphors are figures of speech used for:

- direct comparisons using "like" or "as", for example, "I can run as fast as a hare."
- indirect comparisons sometimes giving human qualities to objects or other living things, for example, "You are a star!"

Question 4

a Identify a simile in the poem.

b Identify **three** metaphors in the poem.

____

____

____

Symbolism is when a feeling, an emotion or an idea is used to represent something else. For example, in the sentence, "He saw red", "red" is associated with anger.

Personification gives human qualities to something that is not human. For example, "the trees whistled in the wind".

Question 5

Re-read **Source 2**, *The Greedy Monster*, and choose the correct response.

a What is the symbolic meaning of the greedy monster in the poem? Circle the answer.

i the importance of sustainability

ii human greed and its destruction on the natural world

iii the need to protect our forests and wildlife

iv include all of the above.

b How does the poet use personification to create a sense of sympathy and support for the natural world? Circle the answer.

i by giving the wind and birds human emotions, such as sadness and sulkiness

ii by describing the forest as being eaten by the greedy monster

iii by creating a sense of atmosphere in the poem

iv include all of the above.

c What message is the poet trying to convey about greed and protecting nature? Circle the answer.

i Greed is destructive for the natural world.

ii We must protect our forests and wildlife.

iii It is important to look after our needs.

iv Include all of the above.

d Which is the most important conclusion being drawn in *The Greedy Monster*?

i We must build more houses.

ii We must protect nature.

iii Greed leads to destruction.

iv Include all of the above.

Literal imagery is when you use words to describe something exactly as it is. For example, "the sky was blue and the clouds were white". Figurative imagery is when you use words to describe something in a way that is not literally true. For example, "the sky was a sea of blue and the clouds were like fluffy white cotton balls".

Question 6

Write one detail from **Source 1** and one detail from **Source 2** that supports this statement, "Trees are important."

Source 1: ____________________

Source 2: ____________________

Question 7

Analyse how the poets in both poems use imagery to convey the importance of protecting nature.

Source 1: ____________________

____

____

Source 2: ____________________

____

____

Question 8

How do the two poems reflect the challenges and opportunities we face in protecting nature in the real world?

____

____

____

Part 2

Question 9

Write a story about a tree that comes to life and talks to a child about the importance of trees and the natural world.

Reflection

Answer these questions once you have completed the task.

- Make a list of three things in this task that you did well.

- What could you do better?

- Write down one thing that you learned in another task that helped you here.

Practice paper 4

This task has two parts. For both parts, you must read **Source 1** and **Source 2**.

- Part 1 has questions 1 to 9.
- Part 2 has question 10.

→ Before you start ...

You need to read the source materials carefully or you will not be able to answer the questions correctly. There are several things that you should pay attention to as you read the texts.

- What kind of writing is it? This will help you decide the writer's purpose.
- What is the main idea? How do I know?
- Who is the intended audience? What evidence can I find to confirm this?

Part 1

SOURCE 1 **Antarctica**

The llama stood on the edge of the cliff, mesmerised by the orca whales swimming in the water below. The penguin was hiding in the shade of a snow dune, hoping to avoid the attention of the leopard seal lurking nearby.

The ice stretched out before the explorers, creating a magical landscape.
The ice glaciers rose like steel-covered valleys, their unforgiving surfaces sculpted by the wind and the cold. The explorers carefully made their way through the treacherous terrain, their hearts beating with excitement.

They had come to Antarctica to study the wildlife and to explore the continent's many mysteries. They were amazed by the beauty and the power of this frozen world.

However, this frozen world has been slowly reducing as global warming and marine pollution impacts its environment.

As they stood on top of a snow-capped mountain, they could see for miles in every direction. The vast white plains were dotted with icebergs that were clearly broken up and becoming part of the sea. Nevertheless, the explorers felt a sense of awe and wonder as they realised how small they were in comparison to the vastness of Antarctica.

They knew that they would never forget their time on this amazing continent.
It was a place of beauty, power and mystery. It was a place that had changed them forever.

SOURCE 2 Jamaica: *A Tropical Paradise*

Introduction

Jamaica is a Caribbean Island known for its beautiful beaches, lush rainforests and vibrant culture. The hottest season in Jamaica runs from June to September, and during this time the weather is sunny and warm, with temperatures averaging around 30 degrees Celsius (86 degrees Fahrenheit).

Enjoy the sun

Jamaica's hottest season is the perfect time to enjoy the island's many beaches. Whether you are looking for a secluded cove or a lively beach party, you are sure to find it in Jamaica.

Enjoy the sand and sea

Some of the most popular beaches include Negril Beach, Doctor's Cave Beach and Seven Mile Beach. The white sand beaches are as soft as powder. The turquoise waters are like a crystal-clear mirror.

Explore the island's natural beauty

Jamaica is also home to a variety of rainforests and waterfalls. The Blue Mountains National Park is a UNESCO World Heritage Site and is home to some of the most spectacular scenery in Jamaica. Other popular natural attractions include the Dunn's River Falls and the YS Falls. The rainforests are as green as emeralds. The waterfalls are like cascading veils of white lace.

Experience the Jamaican culture

Jamaica is known for its vibrant culture, which is influenced by its African, European and Asian heritage. The island's music, food and festivals are all unique and unforgettable. Some of the most popular Jamaican festivals include the Carnival and the Reggae summer festival. The Jamaican music is as infectious as a fever. The Jamaican food is a melting pot of different flavours.

Make the most of your trip to Jamaica in the hottest season by visiting the island's many beaches, exploring its natural beauty and experiencing its vibrant culture.

Question 1

Rewrite these sentences. Use punctuation marks from the box.

a can you hear the thunder and see the lightning

____

b the environment is home to wild animals insects and birds

____

c there are cars lorries and buses speeding past john shouted

____

d listen to the howling wind and the pouring of the rain

Mark	Use	Example
Capital letter	for names at the beginning of sentences	Bob Marley The poem is about acting like a tree.
Full stop (.) Question mark (?) Exclamation mark (!)	at the end of sentences	This is my book. Where is the fire exit? In the event of a fire, you must leave the building immediately!
Comma	to separate words in a list	Birds, insects and snakes live in trees.
Speech marks (inverted commas)	to show that someone is speaking	"Be careful!", Mom shouted.

Question 2

a What do you think it is like to live in Antarctica?

b Can you name any animals that live in Antarctica?

c Compare and contrast the experiences of the llama and the penguin in the passage.

ICT and Geography link: Create a digital travel brochure using Canva or Google Slides. Compare Antarctica and Jamaica – include images, facts and your own captions.

d Explain how the explorers' description of Antarctica creates a sense of awe and wonder.

____

____

____

____

e What does the passage suggest about the impact that Antarctica had on the explorers?

____

____

____

____

Direct speech refers to reporting the exact words of a speaker. For example:

- Statement: Samoy thought it was too dangerous to drive in the bad weather.
- Direct speech: "It is too dangerous to drive in this weather!", she exclaimed.

Question 3

Convert each of the following statements into direct speech.

a Michael was amazed by the beauty and the power of the frozen world.

____

b They had a brilliant time in Antarctica.

____

c They were very cold.

____

d He had forgotten to put on his thick socks.

____

If we report what someone said, we do not use quotation marks. For example:

- Samoy exclaimed that it was too dangerous to drive in the bad weather!
- "It was too dangerous to drive in that weather.", exclaimed Samoy.

Question 4

For each of the following statements, report what is said using an appropriate reporting verb from the box.

remarked	explained	asked	announced

a Teacher: "Rich vegetation prevents soil erosion."

____

b Marsha: "The sights in Antarctica are breathtaking."

____

c News presenter: "All flights are cancelled due to the weather conditions."

____

d Sean: "Where should we go on our next adventure?"

____

Question 5

What do you think the author's purpose is in **Source 1**, *Antarctica*? Explain your reasoning.

____

____

____

____

A simile is a comparison of two things using the words "like" or "as".

A metaphor is a comparison of two things without using the words "like" or "as".

Question 6

Identify three similes and three metaphors in **Source 2**, *Jamaica: A Tropical Paradise*.

a Three similes in **Source 2**.

___

___

___

b Three metaphors in **Source 2**.

___

___

___

Text features are the parts of printed items such as an introduction, a heading, a subheading and a conclusion that help the reader find and learn information easily.

Question 7

Re-read **Source 2**, *Jamaica: A Tropical Paradise*, and identify the text feature where you would find the answer. The first one has been done for you.

a Where would you find information on how Jamaica's heritage has been influenced by others?

Text feature: Heading – Experience the Jamaican culture.

b Where would you find information on a Carnival in Jamaica?

Text feature: ___

c Where would you find information on a world heritage site?

Text feature: ___

d Where would you find information on the best time to enjoy the island's beaches?

Text feature: ___

Figurative language describes the techniques a writer uses to create meaning and have an impact on the reader. For example, "The rainforests are as green as emeralds".

Question 8

a Explain how the author uses figurative language to describe Jamaica's hottest season.

b Analyse the different ways that tourists can enjoy Jamaica's natural beauty during the hottest season.

c Based on your experience or on what you have learned, compare and contrast the different types of food that are served at the Carnival and the Reggae summer festival.

Question 9

Evaluate the different ways that Jamaica's tourism industry benefits from the country's hottest season.

Part 2

Question 10

a Look at this herringbone diagram as a guide for creating a story.

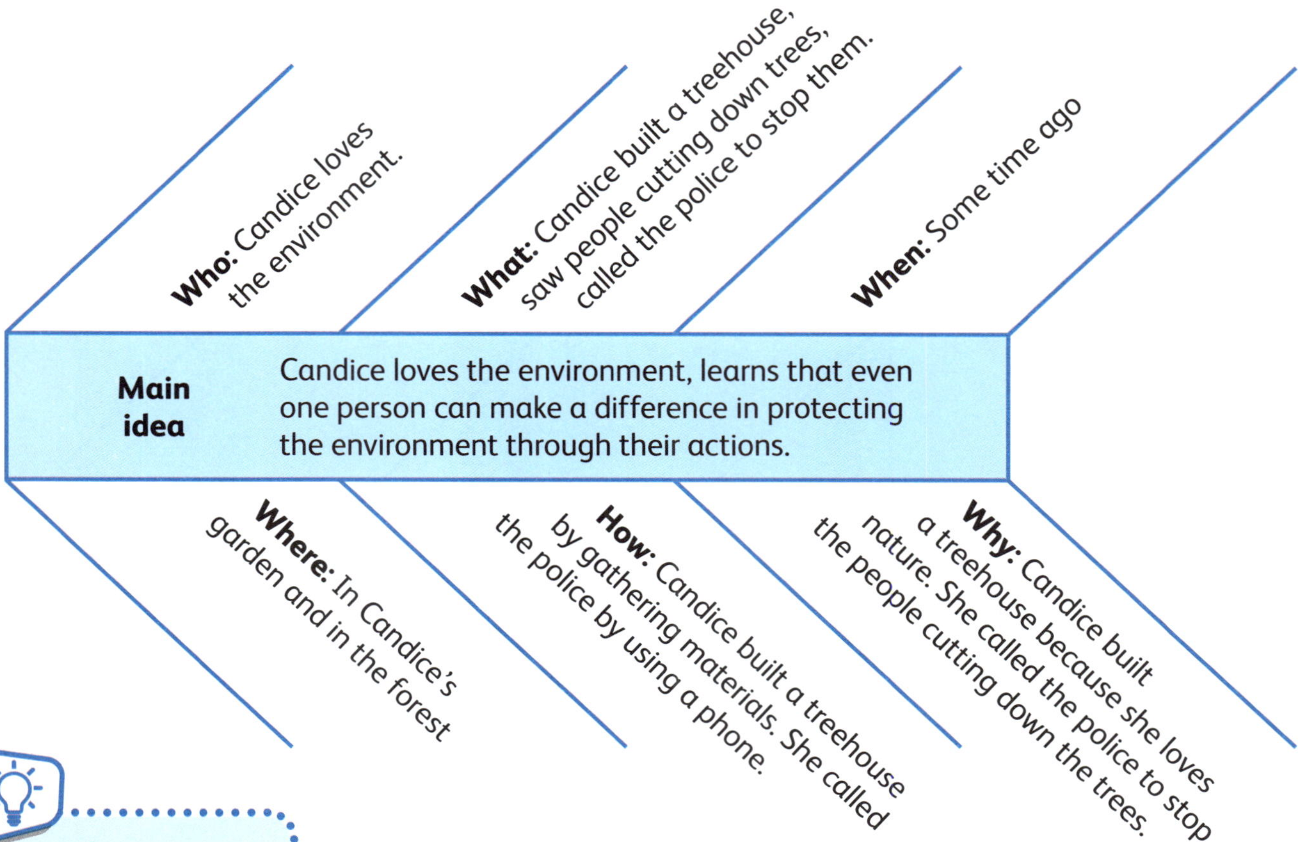

- Think about the different environmental issues that you think are important.
- Consider the different ways that you can tell a story about these issues.
- Use the herringbone diagram to brainstorm new characters, settings, conflicts and resolutions.

b Now read the full story about the environment (including some transitional words) from the herringbone diagram.

Some time ago, there was a young girl named Candice who loved the environment. She built a treehouse in her garden to enjoy nature. One day, she saw a group of people cutting down trees in the forest. Following this, Candice decided to stop them and called the police. Soon after, the police arrived and stopped the people from cutting down the trees. In conclusion, Candice continued to enjoy her treehouse and learned that even one person can make a difference in protecting the environment.

c Create notes using the herringbone diagram for your own story about the environment in Antarctica.

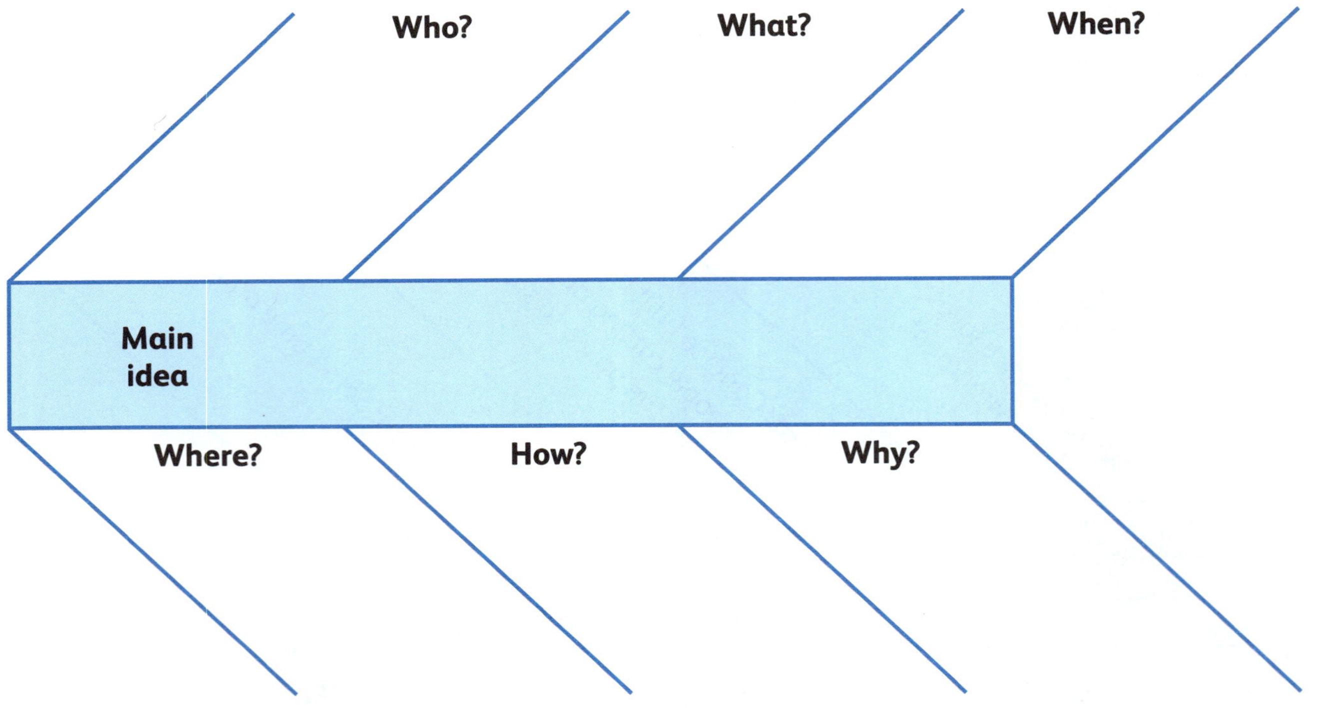

d Write out the full story from your notes in the herringbone diagram. Use some transitional words that will help the reader follow the links between your ideas.

Reflection

Use your answers to the task to assess your own learning.

- List the question numbers.
- Rate your work on each question using this scale:

Question	Below standard	On track	Above standard

Practice paper 5

This task has two parts. For both parts you must read **Source 1** and **Source 2**.

- Part 1 has questions 1 to 6.
- Part 2 has questions 7 to 9.

→ Before you start …

- Read the whole paper carefully.
- Underline all the instruction words, so you know what you have to do.

Part 1

SOURCE 1

Carrots

They say that carrots are good for your eyes,
They swear that they improve your sight,
But I'm seein' worse than I did last night–
You think maybe I aint usin' 'em right?

By Shel Silverstein

SOURCE 2

Health and Well-being

[1]You can improve your general health and well-being if you make healthy food choices and [2]exercise. It is important to develop good eating habits and an awareness of portion control. [3]**These** habits prevent **adverse** health conditions, such as obesity, heart disease and [4]diabetes. **Adopting** healthy eating habits and exercising can also improve mental health, as [5]research suggests it **supports** cognitive function. If your diet includes food from all food groups, this will naturally provide a variety of food and nutrients that the body needs to function properly. An assortment of foods that include meat, fish, eggs, dairy products,

fruit, vegetables and grains, such as oats, are good. It is also necessary to limit foods high in saturated and trans fats and avoid any processed food and drinks with added sugars. A balanced diet will help you grow up strong and healthy, prevent sickness and maintain a healthy weight.

Physical exercise is also necessary and should be part of your daily routine. According to the Ministry of Health and Wellness, Jamaica (MOH), exercising regularly is essential for maintaining good health and well-being, and it can also help manage and reduce the risk of illnesses, such as heart disease, stroke, cancer and diabetes. Physical activity is one of the best ways to stay healthy and live a long life. The MOH recommend that children should do a combination of muscle-strengthening and bone-strengthening activities for 60 minutes at least three times per week.

Question 1

Read the question for key words or key ideas. Then scan (quickly read) both sources.

Write one detail from **Source 1** and one detail from **Source 2** that support the statement that carrots are healthy.

Source 1: ______________________________

Source 2: ______________________________

Question 2

In no more than ten words, write the main idea of **Source 1**, the poem and **Source 2**, the article.

Source 1: ______________________________

Source 2: ______________________________

Question 3

a According to **Source 1**, *Carrots*, circle which statement you think is correct.

i The speaker is certain that carrots are bad for your general health.

ii The speaker is positive that carrots are good for your general health.

iii The speaker is convinced that carrots will improve their eyesight.

iv The speaker is unsure of the benefits of carrots for your health or eyesight.

b According to **Source 1**, *Carrots*, circle which statement you think is correct.

i The speaker has been eating carrots, but their vision has not improved.

ii The speaker wonders mockingly if they are using their carrots correctly.

iii The speaker was brought up to think that carrots are good for your sight.

iv The speaker was raised to believe carrots improve sight but they are doubtful.

Question 4

According to **Source 2**, *Health and Well-being*, circle whether the statement is *T* for True or *F* for False.

a	It is important to be mindful of how much food you put on your plate.	T / F
b	A healthy diet is the only thing you need to improve your mental health.	T / F
c	Unhealthy food choices can increase your risk of developing heart disease.	T / F
d	You only need to eat food from one of the food groups to get all the nutrients you need.	T / F

Question 5

Look again at **Source 2**, *Health and Well-being*, and circle the correct answers.

a The word **These** in line 3 is closest in meaning to:

i habits

ii exercises

iii foods

iv nutrients

b Circle the correct answer. The word **adverse** in line 3 is closest in meaning to:

i favourable | ii unfavourable
iii neutral | iv uncertain

c The word **adopting** in line 4 is closest in meaning to:

i accepting | ii choosing
iii starting | iv considering

d The word **supports** in line 5 is closest in meaning to:

i helps | ii advances
iii sustains | iv maintains

Question 6

Look at the different health conditions that are mentioned in Source 2, Health and Well-being. What do they have in common? The text mentions obesity, heart disease, diabetes and mental health as all being improved by making healthy food choices and exercising.

a **Source 2**, *Health and Well-being*, states that making healthy food choices and exercising can improve your general health and well-being. What can you infer about the relationship between diet, exercise and overall health?

When you infer something, you make a conclusion based on the evidence you find.

b The text mentions the importance of developing good eating habits and portion control. Suggest practical strategies for achieving these goals.

ICT link: You could create a short video advert or jingle promoting carrots as a healthy food. Use a tool like Adobe Express, Canva Video or your phone camera.

c The text states that adopting healthy eating habits and exercising can also improve mental health. What can you infer about the connection between physical health and mental health?

____

____

____

____

d The text mentions that a diet that includes food from all food groups will naturally provide a variety of food and nutrients that the body needs to function properly. What can you infer about the importance of a balanced diet?

____

____

____

____

Part 2

Question 7

How would you identify the components of a story plot? Look at the diagram, then draw a line to match the stages to the correct part of a story in the following exercise.

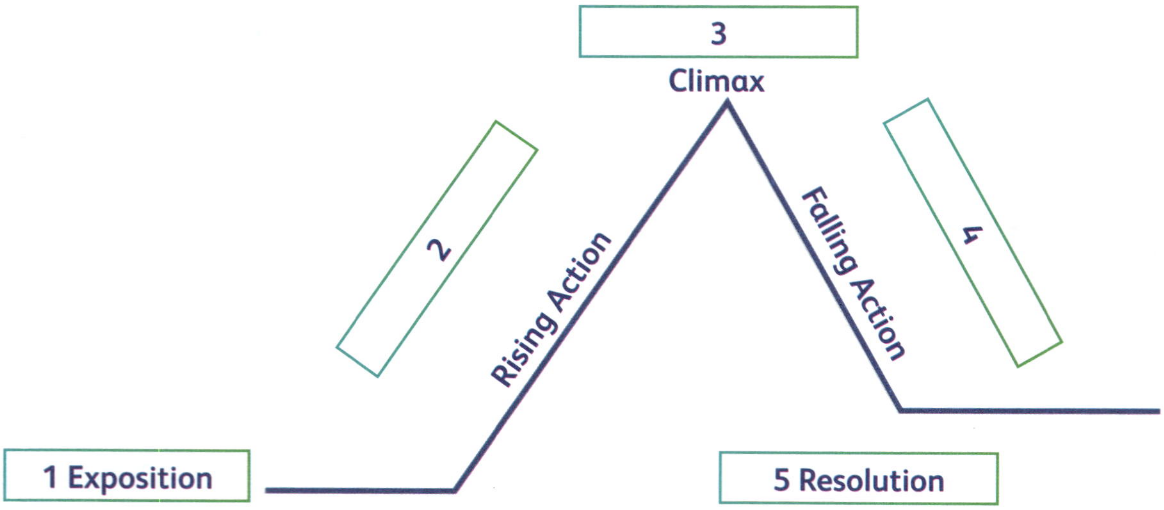

	Stages in the diagram
1	Exposition
2	Rising Action
3	Climax
4	Falling Action
5	Resolution

Parts of a story
the most exciting part of the story when we learn the outcome
end of the story
where the main character faces a series of conflicts
beginning of the story where characters and setting are introduced
events leading to the end of the story

Question 8

Using what you have learned about the different parts of a story, it is time to write your own. Create a short story about a child or animal who hates eating vegetables and exercising until something magical happens and they change their mind.

Question 9

Now complete the template on the next page to briefly explain what happens at each stage of your story.

	Stages in the diagram	What happens
1	Exposition	
2	Rising Action	
3	Climax	
4	Falling Action	
5	Resolution	

Reflection

Can you answer "yes" to all of these questions?

If not, write down what you need to do to change your answer.

- Did I understand all of the questions?

- Did I know what to do to answer them?

- Did I follow the instructions correctly?

- Was my work clear and organised?

- Did I perform procedures accurately?

- Did I explain and justify my answers when asked to do so?

Practice paper 6

This task has two parts. For both parts, you must read **Source 1** and **Source 2**.

- Part 1 has questions 1 to 7.
- Part 2 has question 8.

→ Before you start …

- Skim read all the questions.
- Circle or highlight any instruction words.

Part 1

SOURCE 1 Newspaper article

INTRODUCING JAMAICAN children to healthier meal options through new and varied cooking techniques has become an important objective for chef and entrepreneur Peter Ivey. Ivey's non-profit organisation, Mission Food Possible (MFP), recently revived a campaign to teach school canteen operators how to prepare healthy dishes in different ways.

Ivey, 40, told *The Gleaner* that the major goal of MFP, which he founded in 2017, is to promote food security. A definition of food security is the availability of food and people's ability to access it, afford it and use it effectively. This means making extensive use of local food produce, supporting Jamaican farmers and showcasing healthier meal options than what the population usually consumes.

MFP promotes the support of farmers and of local indigenous foods. "What is challenging is how to change the mindset of our young people who are falling in love with this 'fast food, fried food' kind of mentality and straying away from the food we know is good for us," said Ivey.

The MFP's mission of healthy food promotion included an endeavour earlier in October to teach 25 school canteen cooks from five primary and all-age schools in Westmoreland how to use natural foods to prepare delicious meals.

SOURCE 2 School menu

SCHOOL MENU

Breakfast

- Ackee and saltfish with whole-wheat toast and fresh fruit
- Jamaican oatmeal with berries and nuts
- Hard-boiled eggs with whole-wheat toast and pear

Lunch

- Jerk chicken with roasted vegetables and brown rice
- Stewed fish with whole-wheat pasta and salad
- Lentil soup with whole-wheat bread and fresh fruit

Snacks

- Fresh fruit
- Vegetables and dip
- Whole-grain crackers
- Yogurt
- Nuts

A message from Mission Food Possible

- **This menu is based on local and indigenous foods.** For example, ackee and saltfish, jerk chicken and fish stew are all traditional Jamaican dishes that feature local ingredients.
- **Use healthy cooking techniques.** Cooking methods that use dry heat, such as grilling, roasting and baking, seal in the nutrients of food, preserving the nourishment essential for children's growth. This helps preserve the water-soluble vitamins, such as vitamins C and B, which can be easily destroyed by cooking. Stewing and using the water from cooking is also a good way to preserve nutrients, as the liquid can be consumed along with the food.
- **Limit fried and processed foods.** There are no fried or processed foods on this menu.
- **Include a variety of nutrient-rich foods.** This menu includes a selection of fruits, vegetables, whole grains and lean protein sources.

When the subject is singular, for example, "cat", the verb should be singular too. For example, he (singular subject) cooks (singular verb); they (plural subject) cook (plural verb).

Question 1

Re-read **Source 1**, the newspaper article. Identify the subject in the sentence and then circle the verb that agrees with the subject.

a The children in the canteen (is / are) hungry.

b Peter Ivey (like / likes) cooking healthy meals.

c Ackee and saltfish (go / goes) well with whole-wheat toast.

d MFP (support / supports) local farmers.

Question 2

How does Chef Ivey plan to help Jamaican children eat healthier foods?

____

____

____

ICT and Mathematics link: Use Google Sheets or Excel to create a digital version of the school menu. Add columns to rate each item (e.g. taste, healthiness, local ingredients). Create a chart to show your favourite healthy meals.

Question 3

Re-read the newspaper article and circle the correct answers.

a Who will MFP train to cook the school meals?

i Peter Ivey

ii Ivey's organisation

iii school children

iv canteen staff

b Which of the following is important for food security?

i being able to get the food you need

ii being able to afford the food you need

iii being able to eat the food you need to stay healthy

iv being able to obtain, pay for and eat the food you need

c What is the major goal of MFP?

i to introduce healthier meals

ii to promote food security

iii to support Jamaican farmers

iv to teach healthy cooking methods

Question 4

According to **Source 1**, what is one of the challenges that MFP faces in promoting healthy eating?

Question 5

Explain how the cooking techniques used in **Source 2** help preserve the nutrients in the food.

Question 6

Refer to **both sources** and answer the following questions.

a Compare the two sources in terms of their message about healthy eating in Jamaica.

b What are the differences between the purposes of the two sources?

c How do the two sources differ in terms of their intended audience?

Question 7

What are some ways that students can use the *School menu* to change their own eating habits?

Part 2

Think of a starter and explain why this is a good choice. For example:

Starter: Mini peanut butter lettuce leaf wrap

Stay energised throughout the afternoon! The peanut butter is a good source of protein, while the lettuce leaf is light and crispy. The ingredients are all local foods that are readily available in Jamaica.

Question 8

As head boy/head girl, you must lead a team of students to create a school lunch menu for one day. The menu must have a starter, a main meal and a dessert. You can refer to **Sources 1** and **2** for ideas, but you must not duplicate any of the meals on the *School menu*.

- Your choice of food should be based on the Mission Food Possible campaign for providing food security.
- For each course, you should provide the ingredients and explain why the food your team has chosen is a good choice.
- Use the menu template and **Sources 1** and **2** for guidance.

SAMPLE - ONE DAY SCHOOL LUNCH MENU

Breakfast

Main menu

Dessert

Reflection

Use your answers to the task to analyse your strengths and weaknesses.

- What areas are you good at?

- Which areas require more work?

- What work will you do to improve?

Practice paper 7

This task has two parts. For both parts, you must read **Source 1** and **Source 2**.

- Part 1 has questions 1 to 7.
- Part 2 has question 8.

→ Before you start ...

- Underline the key words in each question. These are clues that tell you what you need to do.
- Highlight any important information that is given in the question. You might need to use this to find the answer.

Part 1

SOURCE 1

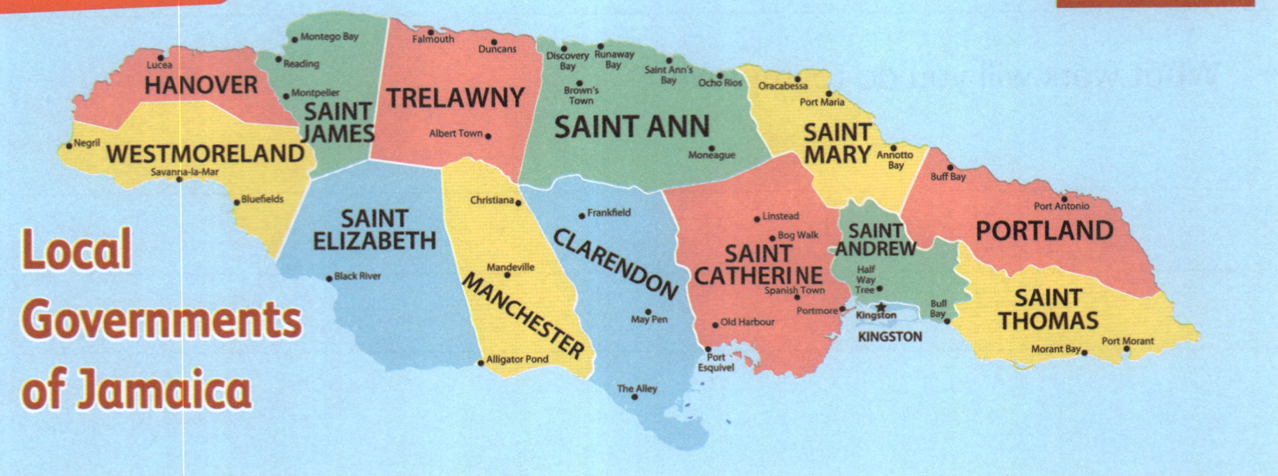

The local governments of Jamaica are responsible for the management of their district. The system is based on the United Kingdom's and is made up of units. These include 14 parishes, two of which are merged into one as the Kingston and St Andrew Corporation. This combining of the two parishes is generally equivalent to the Kingston metropolitan area. Jamaica is also traditionally divided into three counties – Cornwall, Middlesex and Surrey.

Each parish has a mayor who is elected along with councilors so they can oversee welfare services and other programs that help people in their community. In addition, they can make decisions about the management of the town, such as the maintenance of the roads, water supplies, parks and other public facilities. However, agreeing with other parishes in co-ordinating services between different parishes can be problematic.

Local government officials are also responsible for developing renewable energy sources, such as solar and wind power, in a way that is sustainable. This means that energy services can continue to be used by people for a long time without running out of resources. Encouraging the use of public transport and cycling is also important. However, how much to spend and on which services can be difficult to agree on between parishes.

The funding for planning and development of districts come mainly from land taxes and central government grants.

SOURCE 2

St Mary

Original Text	Corrected Text
st mary parish is on the northern part of jamaica	St Mary Parish is on the northern part of Jamaica.
the people of st mary are working together to make a plan for how to develop their community in a sustainable way.	
this means that they want to make sure that their community can grow and thrive for many years to come, without using up all of its resources.	
the government is helping the people of st mary to develop this plan but it is the peoples responsibility to hold meetings and workshops where people can share their ideas.	
the government believes that the people of st mary know best what they need for their community and they want to make sure that everyone has a voice in the planning process.	
the plan will be used to guide the development of st mary for the next 20 years. it will cover things like transportation, education, healthcare and the environment.	
the goal is to create a community that is prosperous, healthy and sustainable for everyone.	

These questions require you to understand and apply the information at a literal level. This means that the information is directly stated in the text without making any inferences or interpretations.

Question 1

Re-read **Source 1**, *Local Governments of Jamaica*, then answer the questions that follow.

a What is the unit of local government in Jamaica?

____

____

b What are the two parish councils that have been amalgamated?

____

____

c What are the two main sources of funding for parish councils?

____

____

d What does the word "merge" mean in the context of the passage?

____

____

e What parishes do the Kingston metropolitan area cover?

____

____

These questions require you to understand information at an inferential level. This means making interpretations and conclusions from the facts and information found in a text, even if they are not obviously stated.

Question 2

a Why do you think the parish councils in Jamaica are based on the system in the United Kingdom?

b What are the possible benefits and challenges of the parish council system in Jamaica?

These questions require you to understand information at a critical level. This means being able to effectively analyse information and form a judgement.

Question 3

a Do you think the parish council system in Jamaica is effective? Why or why not?

b What are some ways to improve the parish council system in Jamaica?

Question 4

a Give two examples of how local governments in Jamaica can plan and develop their local area in a sustainable way.

____

____

____

____

b What are some of the challenges that local governments in Jamaica face in planning and developing their local area in a sustainable way?

____

____

____

____

Question 5

Correct the text in **Source 2**, *St Mary*, writing the correct text in the second column. An example has been done for you. Add capital letters to the beginnings of sentences and to proper nouns. Add other missing punctuation marks, such as periods and commas.

Question 6

a Why is the Jamaican government assisting the St Mary community in developing a sustainable development plan?

____

____

____

____

b What are some of the things that the people of St Mary are considering when developing their plan?

Question 7

According to the sources, who is responsible for sustainability?

Source 1: ______________________________

____

____

Source 2: ______________________________

____

____

Part 2

ICT link: You could create a short video or slideshow using Canva or Adobe Express to present your school's eco-friendly actions. Share with your class or community online.

Question 8

Write a letter to your local council about sustainability and how your school can help. In your letter, you should:

- Define sustainability and explain why it is important.
- Identify some of the ways in which your school is already contributing to sustainability.
- Suggest some specific ways in which your school could do more to promote sustainability.

Follow the basic letter structure in the template. Refer to **Sources 1** and **2** for ideas on sustainability.

Introduction

Dear [Local Council Name]

I am writing to you today to discuss the importance of sustainability and how my school, [School Name], can help.

Body Paragraph 1: Define sustainability and explain why it is important.

____

____

Body Paragraph 2: Identify some of the ways in which your school is already contributing to sustainability.

Body Paragraph 3: Suggest some specific ways in which your school could do more to promote sustainability.

Conclusion: Restate your main points and conclude by thanking the recipient for their time and consideration.

Yours sincerely,

[Your Name]

Reflection

Answer these questions once you have completed the task.

- What evidence shows that I have achieved my aims?

- What did I do well?

- What can I improve on?

Practice paper 8

This task has two parts. For both parts, you must read **Source 1** and **Source 2**.

- Part 1 has questions 1 to 10.
- Part 2 has question 11.

→ Before you start ...

Look at these students' responses for the following question: What is the difference between local and national government? Both students have the right answer, but Annika gets a better grade than Nadia. Can you see why?

Nadia's response	Annika's response
Local government and non-local government are both responsible for making decisions and providing services to the people.	*Local government is responsible for fixing problems in your neighbourhood, such as maintaining parks and streets. Non-local government, such as the national government, is responsible for things like building roads and bridges and making laws for the whole country.*

Nadia does not identify the distinct responsibilities of local and national government and does not provide examples to illustrate the roles of each level of government. Therefore, this is a very basic response.

Annika's response demonstrates a thorough understanding and distinguishes between local and national government responsibilities and provides examples to illustrate the roles of each level of government.

Look at the instruction words and phrases in the Knowledge boxes below. Which Knowledge box goes with Nadia and Annika's responses?

Write either **Recalling information**, **Skills and concepts**, **Strategic thinking** or **Extended thinking** next to their name below. Think about what each instruction means in the Knowledge boxes before you answer the question.

Nadia ______________________________

____

Annika ______________________________

____

Depth of Knowledge

Recalling information	Skills and concepts	Strategic thinking	Extended thinking
Remember, recall, recognise or locate basic details and ideas. There is one correct answer.	Explain, show relationships; use your skills and what you know to make decisions about what to do and how to do it. There is one correct answer.	Explain your thinking and give reasons for your answers. There are different answers and different ways to find the answers.	Plan, think and put ideas together to solve a problem. There are many possible answers and ways of solving the problem.

Part 1

Question 1

What should you do immediately before reading a text to make it easier to understand? Circle the answer(s).

a Preview the text by looking at the title, headings and pictures.

b Think about what you already know about the topic before you start reading.

c Read other texts on the same topic to get more information.

d All of the above are good strategies to use before reading a text.

Question 2

Which of the following strategies is NOT helpful for understanding a text while reading?

a asking yourself questions about the text as you read

b highlighting relevant points

c ignoring the parts of the text that you do not understand

d reading the text slowly and carefully

Question 3

Read the text and answer the following questions.

The Question-Answer Relationship (QAR) is a reading strategy that helps you work out how to ask key questions when reading and how to locate those answers in a text. Begin by looking for answers in the book or text to literal questions and specific facts that are **Right There**. For questions that require deeper analysis, engage in the **Think and Search** mode where answers are found from several parts of the text and draw on inference.
For answers that are not in the text but in your head use the **Author and You** mode where you compare the text to what you already know. When answers are not in the text, use the **On My Own** mode by thinking about what you already know to make connections to the topic.

a What is the purpose of the QAR strategy?

____

____

____

b Explain how the **Think and Search** mode of the QAR strategy is used.

____

____

____

c How can readers use the **Author and You** mode to make personal connections to the text?

____

____

____

d In what situations might a reader use the **On My Own** mode of the QAR strategy?

____

____

____

SOURCE 1

Local Government

Countries in the Caribbean have different systems of local government. **For example**, in some countries, such as Jamaica, people vote for their local leaders. **On the other hand**, in some countries, such as Barbados and Saint Lucia, local leaders are appointed by the central government.

Despite these differences, all local governments in the Caribbean share some common responsibilities. These responsibilities include providing basic services to citizens, such as sanitation, garbage collection, and parks and recreation. **Additionally**, local governments play a role in planning and development, as well as in promoting economic growth and job creation.

Local government is an important part of the Caribbean's democratic system. Indeed, by giving people a voice in how their communities are run, local government helps ensure that everyone has a stake in the future of their country.

SOURCE 2

St Elizabeth Parish

Elizabeth is a parish in southwestern Jamaica. Its capital, Black River, lies at the mouth of the Black River.

It is one of Jamaica's oldest parishes and its first inhabitants were the Taíno people. The Spanish enslaved the Taíno when they arrived in Jamaica, but they left when English settlers arrived in 1655. The parish is thought to be named after Elizabeth Modyford, the wife of Jamaica's first British governor, Sir Thomas Modyford. Some towns in the parish still have Spanish names, such as Santa Cruz.

English settlers developed sugar cane plantations in St Elizabeth, making the parish very prosperous. Black River became an important port for exporting sugar cane, molasses and trees. Other industries, such as cattle farming, papermaking and bauxite mining, developed later.

Many Taíno and Maroon people fled to the hills of St Elizabeth to escape the Spanish and English. They created their own independent communities and built towns such as Accompong. St Elizabethans played an important role in the Sam Sharpe slave rebellion of 1831.

Question 4

Look at **Source 1** and answer the questions:

a What are the two main types of local government systems in the Caribbean?

b What are some of the common responsibilities of local governments in the Caribbean?

Question 5

a What is the main idea of the text in **Source 1**?

b What are some of the ways in which local government can make a difference in people's lives?

Question 6

a Write the transitional word or phrase from the box below next to its definition.

Consequently   As well as   Despite these differences
Additionally   On the other hand   For example

Transitional word or phrase	Definition / Relationship between ideas
	to provide an example
	to contrast two ideas
	to signal a contrast despite previous information
	to show a cause-and-effect relationship
	to add more information to a previous point
	to add more information to a previous point

b Match the transitional words and phrases in Column 1 to their meaning in Column 2. Refer to **Source 1** to read the words in context.

1	For example:
2	On the other hand:
3	Despite these differences:
4	Additionally:

a	This phrase is used to introduce a contrasting point of view, which is that local leaders in some Caribbean countries are appointed by the central government.
b	This phrase is used to add another common responsibility of local governments in the Caribbean.
c	This phrase is used to introduce an example of a different system of local government in the Caribbean.
d	This phrase is used to signal a transition from discussing the differences in local government systems to discussing the common responsibilities of all local governments in the Caribbean.

ICT link: You could use Google Slides or Canva to create an infographic comparing local government systems across Caribbean countries.

Pronouns are used instead of a noun or noun phrase in a sentence.
A pronoun may take the place of the name of a person, place or thing.
Pronoun examples:
I, me, we, they, you, he, she, it, yours, himself, ourselves, its, my, that, this, those, us, who, whom.

Question 7

What pronoun could replace the underlined words?

a Countries in the Caribbean have different systems of local government. ______________

b In some countries, such as Jamaica, people vote for their local leaders. ______________

c Local government is an important part of the Caribbean's democratic system. ______________

d Despite these differences, all local governments in the Caribbean share some common responsibilities.

____

Antecedents are words, phrases or clauses whose place is referred to by a pronoun.
For example, "The dog in the animal shelter is very big, but we still want to adopt it."
The antecedent in the sentence is the underlined word "dog". The sentence continues and then uses the underlined word "it" to refer back to the dog.

Question 8

Circle the duplicated antecedent in each sentence and replace it with a pronoun.

a The mayor attended the mayor's council meeting.

____

b Frank wanted to know where Frank needed to go.

____

c National institutions include government buildings and many politicians visit these National institutions.

____

d The teacher asked the teacher's students to open their books.

____

e The author was proud of the author's book.

____

Question 9

Re-read **Source 2** and circle the correct answers.

a Which of the following is the capital of St Elizabeth parish?

i Santa Cruz
ii Black River
iii Accompong
iv Spanish Town

b Who were the first inhabitants of St Elizabeth parish?

i the Spanish
ii the English
iii the Taíno
iv the Maroons

c Why did the Spanish leave St Elizabeth parish?

i They were defeated by the English.
ii They found new land to explore.
iii They were attacked by the Taíno people.
iv They decided to return to Spain.

d What is the name of the first British governor of Jamaica?

i Elizabeth Modyford
ii Oliver Cromwell
iii Thomas Modyford
iv James II

e What was the main industry in St Elizabeth parish during the colonial period?

i sugar cane production
ii cattle farming
iii papermaking
iv bauxite mining

Question 10

a The text mentions that St Elizabeth is one of Jamaica's oldest parishes. Based on the information provided, what evidence supports this claim? Analyse the text to identify specific details that indicate the historical significance of St Elizabeth as a parish in Jamaica.

b The text discusses the Spanish and English presence in St Elizabeth, highlighting the arrival of English settlers and the development of sugar cane plantations. Evaluate the impact of these two groups on the parish's history and development. Consider both the positive and negative effects of their presence on the parish's trajectory.

____

____

____

____

____

Part 2

Question 11

Write a text about the history of St Elizabeth parish. Be sure to include information about the original inhabitants, the arrival of the Spanish and English and the development of the sugar cane industry.

Follow the framework below for guidance.

Introduction
Begin by introducing the parish of St Elizabeth, mentioning its location within Jamaica.

Original Inhabitants
Acknowledge the Taíno people as the original inhabitants of St Elizabeth.

Arrival of the Spanish and English
Describe the arrival of the Spanish in Jamaica and their subsequent enslavement of the Taíno people.

The Sugar Cane Industry
Mention the sugar cane plantations in St Elizabeth and the significance of Black River as a port.

Conclusion
Summarise the key points about the history of St Elizabeth parish.

> The aim of expository writing is to **inform its reader**. This includes all types of factual writing that is presented in an organised manner and has a clear purpose.

When you write your text, remember to use details in your own words from **Source 2** to support your explanation.

Reflection

Looking closely at your mistakes can help you learn and improve your work. Think about any questions or parts of questions that you got wrong:

- Did you understand the question and know what to do? If not, what can you do about this?

- Did you make any mistakes? If so, what can you do to avoid these mistakes in future?

Practice paper 9

This task has two parts. For both parts, you must read **Source 1** and **Source 2**.

- Part 1 has questions 1 to 8.
- Part 2 has question 9.

→ Before you start ...

Read through all the questions.

- Ask yourself: What am I being asked to do here?
- Jot down your ideas next to each question.

Part 1

SOURCE 1

Broken pipes

Today, I was walking down the street on my way to school when I noticed something strange. First, I heard a loud, unfamiliar noise. Then, I saw it – a massive spring of water shooting high into the air.

"What is that?", I asked some women walking nearby.

"Oh, they are repairing a water main", a woman replied, covering her ears with her hands.

"Don't they know that is disruptive for the community?", I asked surprised.

"Maybe", the woman said. "But what else are they going to do with the water? The pipes are broken and it is flooding the streets."

"What about alternative water sources or installing a better water system?", I suggested.

"Who has time for that?", the woman said, shrugging.

Other people were standing around complaining about the noise and the water damage to their property, another woman complained that her children could not focus on their schoolwork.

I shook my head and continued walking. I did not want to get soaked by the spraying water. I started to wonder how we could solve this problem. What if the water main burst completely? Who would fix it? I decided that we needed to do something about this. As our mayor says, "It is time for action!"

SOURCE 2 The History of Air pollution

Air pollution has been around since the beginning of human history, when people first learned to make fires. In the 1300s, air pollution in England increased due to the growing reliance on coal as a fuel source for both heating homes and cooking food. This resulted in numerous deaths from smoke inhalation. Edward I, the King of England, tried to ban coal burning but failed because coal was cheap and plentiful in England.

Air pollution increased following the Industrial Revolution. Numerous factories were built and large towns developed around them. For instance, the population of Manchester grew significantly between 1801 and 1841. The factories' machinery required a substantial amount of power, while the factory workers needed housing. This increased fuel demand, leading to further air pollution and fatalities as nations industrialised.

SOURCE 3

Technological progress

Progress in technology has allowed us to do more in our everyday lives. We always wish to complete tasks in the easiest and quickest way possible to make our lives simpler and speedier. As a result, we acquire machines to do our tasks for us. Unfortunately, we also use more chemicals, which increases the amount of air pollution emitted into the atmosphere.

Flights, cars, ships, industries, hospitals and the energy required to run our cities all pollute the environment with emissions from burning fuel. Therefore, we must carefully consider the harm we are doing to the air around us. We must do the right thing and consider how to lessen air pollution. According to scientists, for every spacecraft we launch into the atmosphere, over 28 tonnes of the harmful carbon dioxide gas are released as well!

Use quotation marks (" ") when you write to show what people say. For example, "What about banning loud music after 11 p.m.?", I asked.

The quotation marks go at the beginning and the end of the spoken words. The other punctuation marks go inside the quotation marks.

Question 1

Add quotation and punctuation marks where necessary.

a Oh, they are repairing a water main, the woman replied.

b Don't they know that is disruptive for the community I asked, surprised.

c Maybe, the woman said, But what else are they going to do with the water The pipes are broken and it is flooding the streets.

d What about alternative water sources or installing a better water system I suggested.

e Who has time for that the woman said, shrugging.

Question 2

Match the words from **1** to **8** with their correct definition from **a** to **h**.

1	Deforestation:	**a**	The release of a gas or other substance into the air.
2	Emission:	**b**	The process of wearing away the surface of the Earth.
3	Erosion:	**c**	Waste that is thrown away in an improper place.
4	Greenhouse gas:	**d**	The introduction of harmful substances into the environment
5	Litter:	**e**	The contamination of water by harmful substances.
6	Noise pollution:	**f**	The excessive noise that disrupts the environment.
7	Pollution:	**g**	A gas that traps heat in the atmosphere, contributing to global warming.
8	Water pollution:	**h**	The clearing of forests for human use.

Homophones are words that sound the same but have different meanings and spellings.

For example: their = something that belongs to some people – That is their car.

There = a place, where something is – The car is over there.

Question 3

Fill in the blanks with the correct homophone.

a I saw a ____________________ (bare, bear) in the forest.

b The ____________________(sun, son) was shining brightly.

c ____________________ (There, Their, They are) going to the park.

d I ____________________ (hear, here) a bird singing.

e I ____________________ (sea, see) in the distance.

Question 4

Write sentence(s) in your own words which uses each of the following homophones:

a their, there, they are

____

____

____

b your, you are

____

____

c hear, here

____

____

d see, sea

____

____

e pear, pair

Question 5

a According to **Sources 2** and **3**, how do factories and machines contribute to air pollution?

b **Source 2** mentions Edward I's attempt to ban coal burning in England. Why do you think this attempt failed?

c **Source 3** states that we must "carefully consider the harm we are doing to the air around us." What specific examples of activities that contribute to air pollution are mentioned in the source?

d Compare and contrast the writers' perspectives on the role of human behaviour in causing air pollution.

e Based on the information presented in **both sources**, what are some potential solutions to reduce air pollution?

____

____

____

Question 6

Complete the gaps with the correct form of the verb in brackets.

a In the 1300s, air pollution in England ______________ (increase) due to the growing reliance on coal as a fuel source.

b Edward I, the King of England, ______________ (try) to ban coal burning but failed.

c Air pollution ______________ (continue) to increase following the Industrial Revolution.

d The increased demand for fuel ______________ (cause) further air pollution and fatalities.

Question 7

Write five sentences about the picture, using the following verbs in the past simple tense.

go eat play
walk see

____

____

____

____

____

Question 8

Complete the sentences with the correct form of the verbs in brackets.

a Last year, Mr Brown's neighbours were ____________ (complain) about the smoke from the factory in town.

b However, last month they ____________ (make) big fires to burn their rubbish.

c Mr Brown also notices that his neighbours are ____________ (drive) a big car that emits strong gas fumes.

d Mr Brown finds it ____________ (be) ironic that his neighbours complain about one form of pollution but engage in other harmful practices themselves.

e Mr Brown wished that his neighbours would ____________ (consider) the environmental impact of their actions.

Part 2

ICT and Science link: You could use a tool like Scratch to design a future machine that reduces air pollution. Label its parts and explain how it works in a short voice-over or caption.

Question 9

Read **Source 1** about the water leak. Write an email to your parish council. In the email, tell the council what you think the people of your parish, the council and the mayor should do about this.

Dear [Parish Council Name],

Introduction
Explain what you saw.

____

____

____

____

____

Body Paragraph 1

Describe what happened and your conversation. Explain why the water leak and the noise of fixing it is disruptive for the community.

Body Paragraph 2

Suggest some specific ways, giving your opinion on what the local council should do. For example, provide temporary water services during disruptions.

Conclusion

I believe that by working together, we can find solutions to this water leak issue and ensure that our parish remains a safe place for all.

Thank you for your time and consideration.

Yours sincerely,

[Your Name]

Reflection

Can you answer "yes" to all these questions?

If not, write down what you need to do to change your answer.

- Did I understand all the questions?

- Did I know what to do to answer them?

- Did I follow the instructions correctly?

- Was my work clear and organised?

Practice paper 10

This task has two parts. For both parts, you must read **Source 1** and **Source 2**.

- Part 1 has questions 1 to 6.
- Part 2 has question 7.

→ Before you start ...

Look at these students' responses for the following task: What is one thing you can change to save water? Both students have the right answer, but Annika gets a better grade than Nadia. Can you see why?

Nadia's response	Annika's response
One simple thing you can do to save water is to turn off the tap when you are brushing your teeth.	A more comprehensive approach to saving water would be to implement water-efficient appliances and fixtures throughout your home. This could include installing a low-flow showerhead which can reduce water usage by up to 50% and a water-efficient toilet which can use up to 70% less water per flush. Additionally, you could install a rainwater harvesting system to collect rainwater for use in watering your lawn or garden. This can significantly reduce your reliance on community water sources.

Nadia's response provides a simple and direct solution to save water. Annika's response provides a more comprehensive and nuanced solution to save water. It goes beyond simply suggesting a solution and explains the benefits of the solution and how it can be implemented. It also provides additional suggestions for saving water, such as installing rainwater harvesting systems.

Look at the instruction words and phrases in the Knowledge boxes below. Which Knowledge box goes with Nadia and Annika's responses?

Write either **Recalling information**, **Skills and concepts**, **Strategic thinking** or **Extended thinking** next to their name below. Think about what each instruction means in the Knowledge boxes before you answer the question.

Nadia ____________________

Annika ____________________

Depth of Knowledge

Recalling information	Skills and concepts	Strategic thinking	Extended thinking
Remember, recall, recognise or locate basic details and ideas. There is one correct answer.	Explain, show relationships; use your skills and what you know to make decisions about what to do and how to do it. There is one correct answer.	Explain your thinking and give reasons for your answers. There are different answers and different ways to find the answers.	Plan, think and put ideas together to solve a problem. There are many possible answers and ways of solving the problem.

Part 1

ICT link: You could work in pairs to act out the comic strip. Record your performance as a short video using a phone or tablet.

SOURCE 1

Pollution

Pollution makes no contribution to the way we live.
The Earth and sky and water just deserve more than we give.
But you can make the difference and do more than we did.
Yes, you can stop pollution.
If we all do our own small part and throw away our trash,
And keep our streams and rivers clean, it translates into cash.
That we can use to hide refuse, recycling like a flash.
Bad habits cause pollution.

SOURCE 2 Comic strip

Question 1

a Write one detail from **Source 1** and one detail from **Source 2** that supports the statement "pollution is harmful to the environment".

Source 1: ______________________________

Source 2: ______________________________

b Write two ways that students can help reduce pollution based on the information from **both sources**.

Source 1: ______________________________

Source 2: ______________________________

c Both texts mention that bad habits cause pollution. What are some bad habits that contribute to pollution?

____

____

An antonym is a word with the opposite meaning to another.

A homonym is a word that sounds the same as another word and is also spelled the same, but they have different meanings.

For example: **can**. "I **can** sing." In this sentence, **can** means ability.

"I had a **can** of beans on toast." In this sentence, **can** means something made of tin.

Question 2

a How many syllables in each word? Tick [✔] the correct box.

Word	1 syllable	2 syllables	3 syllables	4 syllables
bicycle				
atmosphere				
dirty				
pollution				
water				
solution				
appliances				
conservation				

b Draw lines to match the word and phrases with the correct antonym from the box.

Word
conserve
dirty
solution
turn on

Antonym
clean
turn off
waste
problem

Question 3

Write two sentences for the different meanings of the homonyms.

a saw: 1 ______________________________

2 ______________________________

b bat: 1 ______________________

2 ______________________

c kind: 1 ______________________

2 ______________________

d wave: 1 ______________________

2 ______________________

Question 4

Circle the correct verb.

If the collective noun refers to the group or set as a whole, the verb should be singular.
If the collective noun refers to the individuals in the group, then a plural verb is used.
For example:

"The family is going on vacation next week." (unit)

"The family are packing their bags." (individuals)

"The audience is/are huge."

a The members of the audience (is / are) all clapping.

b There (is / are) a pride of lions at the watering hole.

c The pride of lions (is / are) separating and hunting alone.

d The team of scientists (is / are) doing research in the lab.

e The team of scientists (is / are) arguing about what to do next.

Question 5

a Compare and contrast the content of the two sources. What are the main points that they both make about pollution?

____

____

____

____

b Compare and contrast the organisation of the two sources. How are the ideas presented in each source?

____

____

____

A Venn diagram is made up of two circles that intersect with each other to form a space in the middle. Each circle represents something specific to a category, such as "air pollution" and "water pollution". If there are any pollutants that are responsible for both air and water pollution, they should be written in the middle where the circles intersect (cross over).

Question 6

Look at this list of some of the ways in which pollution is caused. Decide whether each is responsible for air pollution, water pollution or both. Write your answers in the correct spaces in the Venn diagram.

- transportation
- industrial activities
- power plants
- aeroplanes
- agricultural activities
- deforestation
- waste disposal
- household activities, such as the use of air conditioning
- dust from construction activities
- industrial wastewater
- farming runoff, such as fertilisers
- urban runoff from roads, such as oil
- wastewater treatment plants
- oil spills
- waste dumping into bodies of water, such as rivers

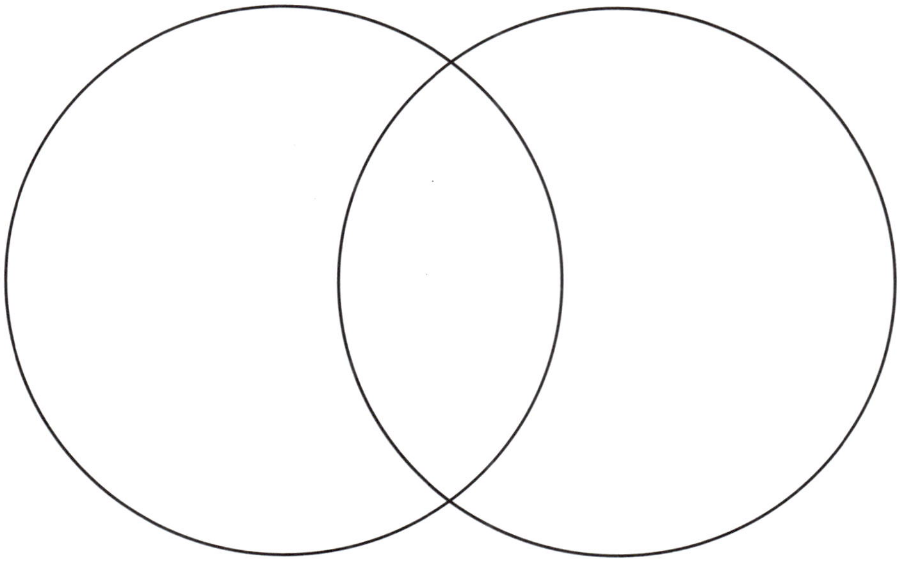

Part 2

Use quotation marks (" ") when you write, to show what people say.

Add text outside of the quotation marks to guide the reader. For example: "What about recycling?", Jayden asked as he was staring at the rubbish.

Question 7

Abigail and Jayden decided to take action to reduce pollution. They started by recycling their rubbish and they encouraged their friends and family to do the same. They also planted trees in their community and they cleaned up their parks and neighbourhoods. As a result of their efforts, they helped make their city a cleaner and healthier place to live. They also inspired others to take action to protect the environment.

Write the conversation between Abigail and Jayden, using the template below. The first two lines have been done for you. Be sure to use information from both sources in your conversation.

Scenario: Abigail is walking down the street and sees her friend, Jayden. They have a conversation about pollution and what action to take to reduce it.
Abigail: "Hey Jayden, have you noticed how polluted our city is becoming?" Jayden: "Yes, it is terrible. The air is like smog and the rivers and streams are full of rubbish." He points to the street floor at some rubbish. Abigail: … Jayden: …

Reflection

Use your answers to the task to analyse your strengths and weaknesses.

- What areas are you good at?

- Which areas require more work?

- What work will you do?